A GIFT FOR:

_____

FROM:

_____

DATE:

_____

Crazy About CHOCOLATE

#1 FOR HAPPY HEARTS!

BARBOUR
PUBLISHING

CRAZY ABOUT CHOCOLATE™

COPYRIGHT © 2004 BY MARK GILROY COMMUNICATIONS, INC.
TULSA, OKLAHOMA

ART AND DESIGN BY JACKSONDESIGNCO,LLC
SILOAM SPRINGS, ARKANSAS

ISBN 1-59310-287-9

All Scripture quotations, unless otherwise indicated,
are taken from the HOLY BIBLE, NEW INTERNATIONAL VERSION®. NIV®.
Copyright © 1973, 1978, 1984 by International Bible Society.
Used by permission of Zondervan Publishing House. All rights reserved.

*Our mission is to publish and distribute inspirational products
offering exceptional value and biblical encouragement to the masses.*

PUBLISHED BY BARBOUR PUBLISHING, INC., P.O. BOX 719,
UHRICHSVILLE, OHIO 44683, www.barbourpublishing.com

 Member of the
Evangelical Christian
Publishers Association

PRINTED IN CHINA.

Crazy About Chocolate

FEW FOODS STIR EMOTIONS AND INSPIRE PASSION AS DOES CHOCOLATE. IS IT BECAUSE OF THE MARVELOUS TASTE AND TEXTURE AS A FOOD—OR IS IT DUE TO ITS LEGENDARY REPUTATION AS AN EMOTIONAL ELIXIR?

WHATEVER IT IS THAT MAKES YOU SO CRAZY ABOUT CHOCOLATE, ENJOY, SAVOR, AND SHARE THE FOLLOWING INSIGHTS, HISTORICAL TRIVIA, QUOTES, HUMOR—AND RECIPES, BOTH SIMPLE AND SOPHISTICATED—DEVOTED TO THE FINE ART OF CHOCOLATE.

ALL I REALLY NEED IS LOVE, BUT A LITTLE CHOCOLATE NOW AND THEN DOESN'T HURT!

LUCY VANPELT

I'M CRAZY ABOUT CHOCOLATE
BECAUSE IT REPRESENTS
LIFE'S GRAND POSSIBILITIES!

I don't know where to begin
but I'm still going to start soon.

Boldly Go

I never met a chocolate I didn't like.

DEANNA TROI
STAR TREK: THE NEXT GENERATION

A Valuable Commodity

A chocolate in the mouth
is worth two on the plate.

I'M CRAZY ABOUT CHOCOLATE
BECAUSE IT IS A PLEASURE
TO CLEAN UP.

Is Chocolate Good for You?

The most extensive medical study of chocolate was done by French doctor Herve Robert, who published the book *Les Veritus Therapeutics du Chocolat*. He posited that chocolate was not a significant cause of such maladies as migraine headaches, acne, obesity, nor tooth decay—common charges from chocolate naysayers.

To the contrary, Robert argued that some of the main components of chocolate—caffeine, theobromine, serotonin, and phenylethylamine—make it a tonic, an antidepressive and anti-stress agent that enhances pleasurable activities.

But very few true chocolate lovers really need such scientific background to know how chocolate makes them feel!

I'M CRAZY ABOUT CHOCOLATE
BECAUSE IT IS ALWAYS
A WONDERFUL GIFT.

(ESPECIALLY WHEN GIVEN TO ME.)

For me? Oh...really, you shouldn't have...

Great Moments in Candy Bar History

The Clark Bar was born in 1917 in Pittsburgh, Pennsylvania.

Goo Goo Clusters were first produced in 1912 by the Standard Candy Company of Nashville, Tennessee. It was the first candy bar to combine milk chocolate, caramel, marshmallow, and peanuts. Because of heat and humidity, the candy is not available during the summer.

Heath Bars were first produced in 1928 by L.S. Heath and Sons, Inc. The candy is currently produced by Hershey Chocolate.

M&M's debuted in America in the 1940s.

The 3 Musketeers bar, introduced in 1932, originally had three distinct parts—chocolate, vanilla, and strawberry. In the 1940s it was changed to its current all-chocolate formula of chocolate nougat completely covered in milk chocolate.

Tootsie Rolls were introduced in 1896 and were named after the pet name of the daughter of their creator, Leo Hirschfield.

Twix debuted in 1977.

During the 1920s nearly forty thousand different kinds of candy bars were made in the United States.

(Oh, for the good old days.)

I'M CRAZY ABOUT CHOCOLATE
BECAUSE IT IS A YEAR-ROUND SPORT.

The Chocolate War

Hershey Kisses were introduced in 1907 and have been pouring out of the factory ever since, with one exception. Production of Kisses was interrupted from 1942-1949, due to the rationing of silver foil in World War II.

However, during this time, the company supplied three billion chocolate bars to the U.S. military.

I'M CRAZY ABOUT CHOCOLATE
BECAUSE IT HELPS CHASE
AWAY RAINY DAYS.

There now, Tabby, storms always pass...

Is There a Substitute for Chocolate?

Carob is a brown powder made from the pulverized fruit of a Mediterranean evergreen. Some consider carob an adequate substitute for chocolate because it has some similar nutrients (calcium and phosphorus), and because it can, when combined with vegetable fat and sugar, be made to approximate the color and consistency of chocolate. Of course, the same arguments can as persuasively be made in favor of dirt.

SANDRA BOYNTON, AUTHOR OF
CHOCOLATE: THE CONSUMING PASSION

I'M CRAZY ABOUT CHOCOLATE
BECAUSE CHOCOLATE IS
CRAZY ABOUT ME.

Never Ever Give Up

I could give up chocolate
but I'm not a quitter.

Chocolate and Long Life

I have this theory that chocolate
slows down the aging process....
It may not be true, but do
I dare take the chance?

I'M CRAZY ABOUT CHOCOLATE
BECAUSE IT'S GREAT FOR SHARING.

True Strength

Strength is the capacity to break a chocolate bar into four pieces with your bare hands—and then eat just one of the pieces.

JUDITH VIORST

A True Friend

There's nothing better than a good friend,
except a good friend with CHOCOLATE.

LINDA GRAYSON, AUTHOR OF *THE PICKWICK PAPERS*

I'M CRAZY ABOUT CHOCOLATE
BECAUSE IT'S PART OF
MY HEALTHY LIFESTYLE.

Lindsey's Six Layer Bars

RECIPE

½ C. MELTED BUTTER

1½ C. GRAHAM CRACKER CRUMBS

14 OZ. SWEETENED CONDENSED MILK

1 C. SEMISWEET CHOCOLATE PIECES

1 C. FLAKED COCONUT

1 C. FINELY CHOPPED NUTS

Pour butter into 16-inch baking dish. Sprinkle with
graham cracker crumbs. Pour condensed milk over crumbs.
Top with chocolate, coconut, and nuts. Press down slightly.
Cook at 325° for 5 to 6 minutes. Cover and let stand for 5 minutes.
Chill, then cut into squares.
Makes 32 bars.

Ruby's Fudge Pie

RECIPE

½ C. MELTED BUTTER

2 SQUARES UNSWEETENED CHOCOLATE

1 C. SUGAR

¼ TSP. SALT

¼ C. FLOUR

2 SLIGHTLY BEATEN EGGS

Melt butter and chocolate on stove. Mix in sugar, salt, and flour, then stir in eggs. Pour into greased pie pan. Bake at 350° for 30 minutes.

Amy's Candy Bar Pie

RECIPE

8 OZ. SWEETENED CHOCOLATE

1 TBSP. WATER

1 TSP. INSTANT COFFEE

8 OZ. COOL WHIP

PIECRUST

Microwave sweetened chocolate for 45 seconds.

Mix with water and instant coffee.

Fold into Cool Whip. Pour into piecrust.

Chill for 1 hour.

Ashley's Cherry Chocolate Cake

RECIPE

1 BOX CHOCOLATE CAKE MIX
1 CAN CHERRY PIE FILLING
2 EGGS, BEATEN

Mix cake mix, pie filling, and eggs together with spoon. Do not beat. Mixture will be very thick. Bake at 350° for 30 minutes.

Frosting:

8 OZ. CHOCOLATE CHIPS	**1/2 C. CREAM CHEESE**
1/2 STICK MARGARINE	**1 TSP. VANILLA**
1 BOX POWDERED SUGAR	**1/2 C. CHOPPED NUTS**

Melt chocolate chips and margarine in saucepan;
let cool. Mix together powdered sugar, cream cheese, and vanilla.
Add chocolate mixture to sugar, cream cheese, and vanilla mixture.
Add nuts and spread on cake.

Bo's Buckeye Fudge

RECIPE

2 3-OZ. PACKAGES SOFT CREAM CHEESE

1 14-OZ. CAN CONDENSED SWEET MILK

2 10-OZ. PACKAGES PEANUT BUTTER CHIPS

Beat cream cheese until fluffy. Beat in milk.
Melt peanut butter chips and stir into mixture.
Chill for 2 to 3 hours. Shape into 1-inch balls.

10 OZ. CHOCOLATE CHIPS

1 OZ. PARAFFIN WAX

Heat chocolate chips and wax together until melted and stir.
Dip peanut butter balls
into chocolate, leaving one small opening.
Let set on waxed paper. Makes 7 dozen.

Greg's Rich Chocolate Cheesecake

RECIPE

16 OZ. CREAM CHEESE

¾ C. SUGAR

½ C. COCOA

1 TSP. VANILLA

2 EGGS

GRAHAM CRACKER CRUST

COOL WHIP

Beat cream cheese, sugar, cocoa, vanilla, and eggs together
until smooth. Pour into graham cracker crust.
Bake at 375° for 20 minutes. Chill for 30 minutes.
Add a dab of Cool Whip when serving.

Shannon's Swiss Mocha Coffee Mix

RECIPE

2 C. COFFEE-MATE

2 C. UNSWEETENED COCOA

1 C. INSTANT COFFEE CRYSTALS

2 C. SUGAR

1 TSP. NUTMEG

1 TSP. CINNAMON

Mix all ingredients. Store in a covered container.

Add 2¾ teaspoons to a cup of hot water.

Top with whipped cream and sprinkle with nutmeg.

Put in a decorative tin, this mix makes a great gift for neighbors during Christmas holidays.

Genevieve's Giant Chocolate Chip Cookie

RECIPE

1 BOX YELLOW CAKE MIX

1/2 C. OIL

2 TBSP. WATER

2 EGGS, BEATEN

1 C. CHOCOLATE CHIPS

Combine ingredients and stir until moistened.

Place on a lightly greased pizza pan.

Bake at 350° for 20 to 25 minutes or until golden brown.

Zach's Hot Fudge Sauce

RECIPE

1 C. SEMISWEET CHOCOLATE PIECES
1/2 C. LIGHT CORN SYRUP
1/4 C. HALF-AND-HALF
1 TBSP. BUTTER
1 TSP. VANILLA EXTRACT

In small glass bowl combine chocolate and corn syrup. Heat at low temperature for 4 1/2 minutes. Stir once. Gradually add half-and-half. Stir until smooth. Stir in butter and vanilla.

Variation:
For chocolate mint sauce use 3/4 tsp.
mint extract in place of vanilla.

Caroline's Chewy Fudge Cookies

RECIPE

1 BOX CHOCOLATE CAKE MIX

2 EGGS, BEATEN

½ C. OIL

1 C. CHOCOLATE CHIPS

½ C. CHOPPED WALNUTS

Combine cake mix, eggs, and oil in mixing bowl. Stir with spoon.
Add chocolate chips and walnuts; stir. Shape dough into 36 balls.
Place 2 inches apart on cookie sheets. Bake at 350°
for 10 to 12 minutes. Cool 1 minute on baking sheet.
Remove to cool or eat while warm.

Analucia's Chocolate Oatmeal Cookies

RECIPE

2 C. SUGAR

½ C. UNSWEETENED COCOA

1 STICK BUTTER OR MARGARINE

½ C. MILK

½ C. PEANUT BUTTER

3 C. OATMEAL

1 TSP. VANILLA

Mix sugar, cocoa, butter, and milk in a saucepan.
Boil for 1½ minutes. Remove from heat. Add peanut butter,
oats, and vanilla. Mix well. Spoon onto waxed paper and let cool.

Merrick's Chocolate Coins

RECIPE

2 1/4 C. ALL-PURPOSE FLOUR

1 C. SUGAR

1/3 C. UNSWEETENED COCOA POWDER

1/2 TSP. BAKING POWDER

1 1/4 TSP. CINNAMON

8 OZ. BUTTER (UNSALTED)

1 LARGE EGG, ROOM TEMPERATURE

2 TSP. PURE VANILLA EXTRACT

4 OZ. BITTERSWEET CHOCOLATE, FINELY CHOPPED

Blend flour, sugar, cocoa powder, baking powder, and cinnamon. Cut butter into small pieces and add to mixture. Blend until butter is in small pieces. Lightly beat egg with vanilla, and blend into mix along with the chocolate.

Divide dough in half, and make two "logs"— about 8 inches long and 2 inches wide. Wrap in waxed paper and chill in freezer for 40 minutes.

Adjust racks to upper and lower thirds of the oven and preheat to 350°. Line 3 cookie sheets with parchment paper. Slice dough into ¼-inch-thick coins and place on sheets 2 inches apart.

Bake cookies for 5 minutes, then switch racks and bake 5 more minutes, or until cookies are set. After cooling, store at room temperature in airtight container. Yield: 5 dozen cookies.

Marjorie's Molten Chocolate Cakes

RECIPE

1 TBSP. MELTED BUTTER (FOR PANS)

8 OZ. BITTERSWEET CHOCOLATE, FINELY CHOPPED

4 OZ. BUTTER, UNSALTED

1½ TSP. INSTANT ESPRESSO POWDER

¼ TSP. SALT

6 LARGE EGG YOLKS, ROOM TEMPERATURE

⅓ C. SUPERFINE SUGAR

1 TSP. PURE VANILLA EXTRACT

½ TSP. CHOCOLATE EXTRACT

2 LARGE EGG WHITES, ROOM TEMPERATURE

⅛ TSP. CREAM OF TARTAR

Butter six 4¼-inch tart pans with removable bottoms. Melt chocolate and butter together in double boiler set. Stir frequently. Blend in espresso powder and salt. Cool briefly.

Whip egg yolks and sugar until pale yellow, about five minutes. Blend in vanilla and chocolate extracts. Fold one quarter into chocolate mixture. Whip egg whites until frothy. Add cream of tartar and whip until soft peaks form. Fold into the chocolate mixture. Evenly divide mixture into the tart pans, filling three-quarters full. Cover tightly with plastic wrap and chill for 1 hour.

Preheat oven to 400°. Bake on center rack for 10 to 11 minutes, until edges are set and centers are still soft. Cool for 2 minutes and gently remove from pans onto individual serving plates. Garnish with homemade whipped cream and berries!

Chocolate and the State of Industry

If not for chocolate, there would be no need for control top panty hose. An entire garment industry would be devastated.

Men vs. Women

Man cannot live on chocolate alone;
but woman sure can.

I'M CRAZY ABOUT CHOCOLATE
BECAUSE MY FRIENDS AND
I AGREE—IT IS THE LONG
LOST FIFTH FOOD GROUP.

The Season for Chocolate

As with most fine things, chocolate has its season. There is a simple memory aid that you can use to determine whether it is the correct time to order chocolate dishes: any month whose name contains the letter A, E, or U is the proper time for chocolate.

SANDRA BOYNTON

I'M CRAZY ABOUT CHOCOLATE
BECAUSE IT MAKES CLOSE
FRIENDS EVEN CLOSER.

A World Chocolate Vacation

For the truly crazy chocolate lovers,
here are four chocolaty locations
to visit on your next vacation:

HERSHEY TOWN, USA

HERSHEY, PENNSYLVANIA

Explore the art of chocolate making
and enjoy the Hershey Museum in
"the sweetest place on Earth."

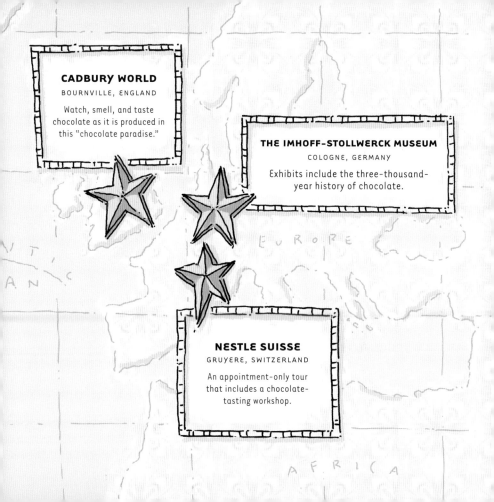

CADBURY WORLD
BOURNVILLE, ENGLAND

Watch, smell, and taste chocolate as it is produced in this "chocolate paradise."

THE IMHOFF-STOLLWERCK MUSEUM
COLOGNE, GERMANY

Exhibits include the three-thousand-year history of chocolate.

NESTLE SUISSE
GRUYERE, SWITZERLAND

An appointment-only tour that includes a chocolate-tasting workshop.

I'M CRAZY ABOUT CHOCOLATE
BECAUSE IT PROMOTES FORGIVENESS
AND HEALTHY RELATIONSHIPS.

Chocolate in England

The Cadbury brand, founded by John Cadbury in Birmingham, England, has been producing chocolate since 1824. As Quakers, the Cadburys were concerned with working conditions not only at their facility, but at the Portuguese cacao plantations on the African islands of Príncipe and São Tomé from which they bought their cacao beans. In 1909, they refused to buy cacao from the slave plantations until working conditions were improved.

The June 6, 1657 issue of the London publication *Public Advertiser* contained the first notice of chocolate for sale in England, 130 years after it was first brought to Spain: "In Bishopsgate Street, in Queen's Head Alley, at a Frenchman's house, is an excellent West India drink, called Chocolat, to be sold, where you may have it ready at any time; and also unmade, at reasonable prices."

Britain spends more per person on chocolate than any other country in Europe—the equivalent of more than $100 per person.

I'm sorry...hold on...I know I have
a couple more pennies in here somewhere...

I'M CRAZY ABOUT CHOCOLATE
BECAUSE IT FITS EVERY BUDGET.

DAILY ☆ TODAY! ☆ TIMES

THE START OF A NATIONAL PASSION

The United States candy bar business blossomed after World War I because the returning soldiers had developed a fondness for the chocolate bars they had eaten as part of their field rations.

Does anyone want to sit down for a snack?

I'M CRAZY ABOUT CHOCOLATE
BECAUSE IT BRINGS PEACE
TO THE FAMILY.

LIFE IS LIKE A BOX
OF CHOCOLATES—
YOU NEVER KNOW
WHAT YOU'RE
GOING TO GET.

FORREST GUMP

IF LIFE IS LIKE A BOX
OF CHOCOLATES,
THEN IT'S TIME FOR ME
TO BUY ANOTHER BOX.
I SEEM TO HAVE
ALREADY DEVOURED
ALL THE GOOD ONES!

I'M CRAZY ABOUT CHOCOLATE
BECAUSE IT PUTS ROMANCE IN THE AIR.

The Mayas and Aztecs
and Chocolate

In A.D. 600 the Mayas migrated from Guatemala to the Yucatán peninsula in Mexico, and establish cacao plantations. It is believed they had cultivated the crop for at least a thousand years on a smaller scale.

The Aztecs conquered the Mayans by the thirteenth century and chocolate was one of their key crops and currencies. Their word for the cacao bean is *cacahuatl.* The word chocolate derived from the Aztec word *xocoatl,* the word for a drink made from cacao beans.

The Aztec ruler Montezuma, at the height of his power, drank as many as fifty cups of chocolate a day!

I'M CRAZY ABOUT CHOCOLATE
BECAUSE IT HELPS WARM
MY HEART DURING THE HOLIDAYS.

I'M CRAZY ABOUT CHOCOLATE
BECAUSE IT MAKES SUCH
A WONDERFUL REWARD.

You met your goal... and here's
that little treat you promised yourself...

When I have Grandma's fudge,
I miss her so much...

I'M CRAZY ABOUT CHOCOLATE
BECAUSE IT HELPS ME REMEMBER
THE PEOPLE I LOVE.

I'M CRAZY ABOUT CHOCOLATE
BECAUSE IT IS ONE OF
GOD'S SPECIAL GIFTS.

EVERY GOOD AND PERFECT GIFT IS FROM ABOVE, COMING DOWN FROM THE FATHER OF THE HEAVENLY LIGHTS. . .

JAMES 1:17

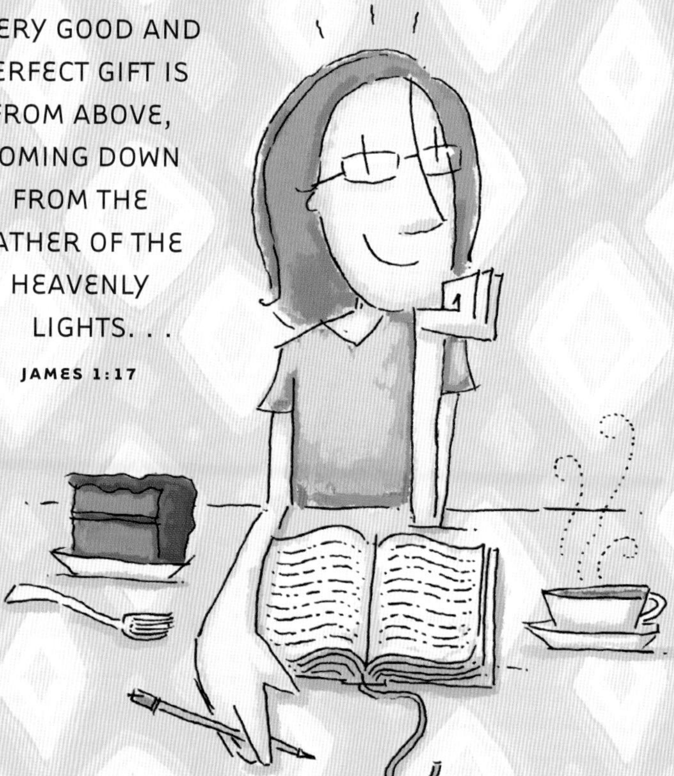

The Crazy Series

Crazy About Christmas
Crazy About Mistletoe
Crazy About My Cat
Crazy About My Dad
Crazy About My Daughter
Crazy About My Dog
Crazy About My Friend
Crazy About My Grandparents
Crazy About My Husband
Crazy About My Mom
Crazy About My Sister
Crazy About My Teacher
Crazy About My Wife
Crazy About You